VENERATED OBJECTS

VENERATED OBJECTS

A collection of poems and short stories

ANDREW V. ZOURIDES

iUniverse, Inc.
New York   Bloomington

Venerated Objects
A collection of poems and short stories

Copyright © 2009 Andrew V. Zourides

iUniverse books may be ordered through booksellers or by contacting:

iUniverse
1663 Liberty Drive
Bloomington, IN 47403
www.iuniverse.com
1-800-Authors (1-800-288-4677)

ISBN: 978-1-4401-9060-5 (pbk)
ISBN: 978-1-4401-9061-2 (ebk)

Printed in the United States of America

iUniverse rev. date: 11/20/2009

I was born in 1951, in the Belmont section of the Bronx, New York. It was a tight knit working class Italian neighborhood, a few blocks from the Natural world of the Bronx Zoo and Botanical Gardens. I was the hybrid of Greek-Italian American parents. My father was hard working, practical and resolute. My mother and sister, free thinking and artistic. My childhood memories reside there until our move in 1965 to the brave new world of Flushing, Queens. The move from the Bronx, from familiar friends and surroundings, prompted my venture into writing poetry, many of which were published many years later. I attended Queens College in 1969, majoring in Art History, then years later, moving to Forest Hills, New York. A few years later I started a clothing business partnership and also met my then life partner, James. It was an 18 year relationship until his untimely death from bone cancer in 1995. He was 41 years old. My poem; "Walking With You" deals with that devastating loss and was written shortly after his death. I gave N.Y.C. and myself a year to decide whether to live in the shadow of what was, or to begin a new life. That new beginning would be Provincetown, Massachusetts, a small art community resort. Provincetown precariously juts out into the Atlantic, at the very last tip of Cape Cod. There, in winter isolation, I made peace with myself and after six years, again ventured forth. I now reside in New Hope, Pennsylvania with my partner, David. Again, near a body of water: the Delaware River. Occasionally, I will hear what sounds like the cry of a seagull, and pretend that the scent of salt air fills my nostrils, and the taste of salt is upon my lips.

To my loving parents, Theresa and Victor and sister Gerry.

To the memory of James, and to David, for both their love and support.

CONTENTS

Titled: "The Journey"
Painting by Andrew V. Zourides

Walking With You

I close my eyes
I see you that last summer.
Your back towards me.
Bright white sand against a cloudless sky.
Nestled safely in your sandy seat
you're held captive by the moving images before you.

I hear your laughter in my silence.
Your shoulders shrugged in exhilaration
with your arms tensed in your lap
Just as that photo of you as a child
as you grasp the chair's edge
with both strong hands.

Your robe falls gently around my shoulders
a bit long on the cuff
and cool to the touch but still familiar.
Alone in the dark
It now shares my side of the bed
finding myself tangled in its embrace.

In my haste, I've opened your small grey bag.
Unzipped, it opens like a paper cut.
Streaked with toothpaste
And filled with the scent
Of hospital soap and disinfectant.

I search nervously through your shaving regimen
Your semblance of health in the mirror.
There pressed against your razors
a small felt medallion of Mary stating "Pray for Us".
Carefully again I place it with the others
and quickly pull the zipper closed.

Photo by Andrew V. Zourides

The Mirrored Ball

Strange as I stand here now
under a pulsating light,
a deafening drone.
I stood here, a young man
some thirty years ago.
The music seemed sweeter,
more connected then.
The glass mosaics
sparkled in their sphere
swirling in their darkening void.
Capturing a face
An exhilarated smile.
Reflecting its image
for a brief moment
Then disappearing forever.

The Pines Tea Dance/ Fire Island/ Summer of '82

There we were
Us and Them.
Tea with a decided twist
of high testosterone.
She in her spiked heels
he in his Swagger.
They all watched across
the dividing line.
Red flags unfurled,
they hurled the ice
from plastic cups.
Fished out by thick fingers
up to the balcony
of Drag Queens.
Like weapons.
Shards of delicate thin glass
slicing across
a brilliant blue sky.

Painting of "Judgement Tarot" by David Rivera

Wings of Desire

The streets were wet and steaming.
Green neon mixed with the scent of Eastern spices.
I took solace from the steady flow
of push and shove
of Main Street Flushing, Queens.
I entered a store bright
with the fluorescent glow of angels.
Row upon row
they beckoned.
With open plastic arms.
In flowing robes of pink and blue icing
marked $9.99
They whispered softly in my ear:
"I will protect you from harm
always…
money back guaranteed".
Suddenly
a box fell from the shelf,
breaking the sacred silence.
In a strident voice
a woman exclaimed:
"Do you have a fresh one?
This one is missing an arm".

Thirst

Because he loves you
Because he drinks
Because you hide the liquor
behind the sink.
It really stinks
praying he will stop,
before the other
vomit stained shoe does drop.
Because he sits
and stares in space
and shouts obscenities
in your face.
Because you love him
Because you care
You wipe the warm urine
from his chair.
And pull his head
out from the john.
To find any recognition gone.
You now sit there
in *his* chair
Fragrant incense
fills the air.
The liquor's gone
He doesn't drink
No empty bottles in the sink
Just the smell of coffee
in the pot
For now, will be
the only thirst
he's got.

Illustration by Andrew V. Zourides

HELP ME!!!

There are always flies.
Flies that settle
on an unfinished sandwich
at a crime scene,
huddled on the perimeter
of the victim's blood.
Flies that sip
into the sweat
of a stand up comedian.
As he slowly bombs
in front of an embarrassed,
shifting audience.
Flies that gorge
on the congealed remains
of strained peas
on the rim
of a child's high chair.
Flies in the eyes
of an Ethiopian child
at daybreak.
There will always be flies.
But then again,
there will always be the spiders
who eat them.

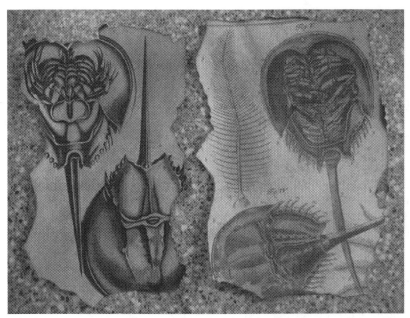
Vintage Etching of a Pair of Horseshoe Crabs
Public Domain courtesy of Vintage Printables

Venerated Objects

There the children stood,
a circle in the sand.
Like warriors in miniature,
prodding
the overturned horseshoe crab.
Its ancient claws playing
a popsicle stick in cadence
to an unforgiving sun,
and screams of laughter.
On the beach that day,
my mother stood
at the blanket's edge.
Chanel mixed with Coppertone,
and Technicolor lipstick
against an olive skin.
"Be careful" she would say,
"Be careful and stay close to the water's edge".
Later, there I found the horseshoe crab:
a victim of play.
Now split in half,
carelessly floating by the water's edge.
Amidst the end of a day's debris,
And a cherry popsicle stick.

Trick

Silently sweeping
across my skin
the coarse
facial hairs
of his shadow
2 A.M.?
secretly
ever so gently
catches my skin
as if dragging
a weight
along the ocean floor.
The taste
of salt
upon his lips
turns to rust
as blood
creeps
between my teeth
and panic
mixed with a tall glass
of peroxide
is served up
with milk and cookies.

Rust

It was late September,
late in the afternoon
by a calm grey sea
in Provincetown.
The tourists had fled
in one grand swoop
after Labor Day.
Swept away
by hard rains
and a mean wind.
I found myself alone
at the playground
at Provincetown's end
swirling round and round
on a child's ride.
Five seats facing
a spiraling center.
I gripped the rusted bar handle
and faced the remaining seats.
The iron rods
creaked and swirled
under my weight.
A counterpoint to the rhythm
of breaking waves.
As a child
On Coney Island's Merry-Go-Round
I sat high
on a fierce galloping horse.
My head precariously forward,
I stared
into his wide glass eyes
and flaring nostrils,
punctuated by throbbing veins.
The sea air
carrying with it
the fragrance of
grilled franks
and densely rich
buttered popcorn.
Suddenly my stash of coins
flew outwards from my pockets
Cascading to the playground's
concrete below,
then breaking my reverie.
Again I was back at the sea
but many years older.
Full circle
as the ride creaked to a stop.

Painting by Gerry McEntegart
Titled: Gargoyles

David's Island

There is an island in view
from the edge of a rattling, angry bridge
in the wilds of Lambertville, New Jersey.
An island
silent, secret and contained.
Where forgotten concrete benches
submerged and drowned
by a fickle River God
occasionally become
the fallen idols of a lost Atlantis.
Where the Goddess dwells
And holds her breath
As she succumbs
to the rising waters.
His island.
David's island.
Frail, and cut by the wind.
It sits.
Steadfast and immobile.

By a Thread

What if
you woke up the next day
and the world had changed?
The key didn't fit.
Your bed was upright
facing Gravity?
What would you do?
Would you pray
that the darkness went away
while the world
lay witness
to a blinding
flash of light?

Photography by Andrew V. Zourides

Theresa in December

My father has a small blackboard
in the kitchen.
Carefully written in chalk,
it simply states:
"My God, Theresa. Where are you?"
"I miss my Theresa".
My mother died that October in 1997.
A decade has passed and everything is still
steadfastly
in its place.
It seems as if
by a sudden whim
she left on an urgent errand,
and would shortly return,
bundles in hand.
I notice the bright blue ceiling
has been repainted.
The smooth enamel paint
obliterating
the tar stained corner of the kitchen,
where she smoked
and collected her thoughts
of remorse and anger.
Her world had been confined to that room.
In years past,
she danced barefoot there.
From cha cha chas
to Motown
to Strauss waltzes.
She glided passed the gleaming utensils
on her newly waxed floor.
It's midnight now.
My father argues with the plastic radio
that fills the room
with the larger world picture
of politics and murder.
At times he clutches her hand
upon his waking dream,
and then writes down
his thoughts and fears
in a little black book.

City

Small child
looking from her window.
Humming to the music of the el train
now in flight.
Caressing a plastic doll
whose eyes are filled
with candy.
Old man
gazing from his window.
Confronted by a brick wall
painted Forest Green.
Sits silently alone
waiting
for the echoes of the voices
from the street below.
Across the half lit shaft,
seeing her small round face
pressed against the glass,
he barely waves to her
before she returns
to a darkened room.
Pleased, he slowly grasps
the glass of scotch and soda
bringing it carefully to his lips.

Photography by Andrew V. Zourides

Crete

We walked together.
My father and I.
Up the bleached hillside
to the rock-hewn church.
The air held its sweet, uncomfortable scent,
hovering closely to our faces.
We ascended:
A pilgrimage to his childhood.
His son following hurriedly
in his footsteps.
The doors swung gently open.
Its secret revealed.
A thousand years
of saints and incense.
Glittering
Flickering
upon its darkened walls.
Whispering to me their secrets
as I told them mine.

Vintage Etching of Monkeys
Public Domain courtesy of Vintage Printable

Do Not Feed The Monkeys

In my childhood of the 1950's, the Bronx Zoo was a familiar, but exotic, escape from the faded brick buildings of the past century, to the paved lots of an uncertain future. Dressed all in our Sunday best, my parents would take me there to see the captive animals. There, I would witness a boundless Nature confined to rusted cages, where neurotic monkeys would glare at us and shout obscenities. I secretly knew their miserable fate and would recall a particular Twilight Zone episode, where *we* were the captives on display, for a cruel, but curious, alien race.

We then would casually parade to the bird section of the zoo, snacks and camera in hand, while the chirps and shrieks of our feathered friends came closer, until the sound became a deafening shrill. The birds didn't have it much better. Though the ancient Victorian birdcages were many times my height, I could still see the delicate tufts of their rainbow colored feathers, impaled on the barbed edges of their lofty cages. I also knew that this was a deliberate clue that was left, from their planned, but failed attempts at escape.

Through the years, in my confused dreams, I came upon those very cages, now empty and silent. As I ate my salted peanuts and sipped my sugary soda, their pungent smells would remind me of the previous tenants. Recently I returned there, to the Zoo's grand parking lot, where the huge baroque fountain was all sunlit and gleaming and profuse with many fragrant flowers. Animals now roamed free, in open, yet contained, contrived environments. We watched them from cute monorails that I had first experienced at the 1964 World's Fair in Flushing, Queens. We now snaked through the plains of Africa and the rain forests of South America. Occasionally, I caught glimpses of the faded and worn brick buildings, peeking through the dense jungle growth. The years had radically changed the face of the Bronx and my neighborhood, but then again, I had also changed along with it.

Now, with a morsel of pretzel in my hand, I boldly tossed it to a group of monkeys…only to have it bounce back from the plate glass window, and fall to an army of ants.

Painting by David Rivera
Titled: Incubus

GOTHIC

The newspaper ad read: "1969 Corvette Stingray Coupe, black exterior/ interior, 428 cubic engine V8, and 82,000 miles. Contact owner." The ad gave a New York upstate phone number. No price or condition of the car was even mentioned. This piqued Jim's curiosity as he had always loved the 1969's aggressive, menacing quality which reminded him of the dark Bat mobile he watched race through Gotham on television some thirty years ago. And of course it *was black...*

His call took him, that cold October, to Saugerties, a town near Woodstock. He drove up slowly to a 1930's Tudor that once, in its time, had a grand edifice, but now was sadly neglected. The driveway was cluttered with leaves and branches that snapped under the wheels of his blue Saturn.

The owner was an odd man, in his late fifties, who gave short quick answers to Jim's queries about the Corvette: all with no elaboration and virtually no eye contact, and certainly not a man anxious to sell such a hot and desirable car. The quoted price surprised him as very reasonable and Jim stipulated that he needed to send over a mechanic to examine the car before he would close the deal. The man agreed, and several days later after arrangements could be made, the car was his.

Jim was a quiet man, gay, but conservative in dress and manner. In all his 42 years, he was still a man who kept his physique toned and his appearance still turned heads. His recent breakup had found him alone, longing for a new identity and self awareness.

The Saturn, his daily driver and now orphaned, sat in the driveway while the Stingray in all its powerful and threatening glory, now had a place of honor in the heated garage.

That night, he sat in the car transfixed by the sleek cockpit and raked seats. Suddenly, he felt that he was not alone and some inexplicable presence hovered warm and close to his right ear. The rear view mirror had a slice of light momentarily and he felt the sudden onset of confusion and fear of what he could be imagining. After all, it was a rather stormy October night outside and he was alone and in partial darkness. He overcame his anxiety, as he was a rational man, and he decided to take it for a spin tomorrow night after work.

Jim had a restless sleep that night, imagining himself in the Stingray but this time it was different. The low voice of a man now whispered against his ear, darting his tongue in and out, while gripping his neck tightly, and painfully towards him. He could see the man in the rear view mirror as he clutched his head. He found that he could not move his hands from the steering wheel, no matter how he tried. The dark figure stopped for a moment, and turned his gaze towards the mirror and catching Jim's eyes, grinned sardonically, never letting Jim out of his vice like grip he held around his neck. It was dangerously exciting as his tongue raced over and behind his neck, and hotly around his chest and down to his groin.

He woke up startled by the dream, and in a frantic moment, touched his ear which was still wet and warm. His neck was irritated as if by a tight collar or coarse rope. He lay there, aroused, but wary of what had transposed. Feeling weak and thirsty, he went downstairs, had a glass of water and went promptly back to bed.

The next morning he found it difficult to get out of bed and had to cancel his appointments with his clients. The next day, and the next, followed a similar pattern and by the end of the week, Jim found himself unshaven and unkempt. The Stingray though, had been polished to a high sheen by him while he was still in his bathrobe and slippers. He had now become overtly obsessed with the car and spent hours in the driver's seat, sometimes sleeping overnight, in the hope that the dream, and the man, would appear to him again. The dream and the man usually did, but with each occurrence it became more intense and violent. He was becoming increasingly bruised around the neck and ear and he was aware that something <u>had</u> to be done. He reluctantly put out an ad to sell the car and hopefully, at least, recouped his losses.

The ad came out that week and simply read:

"1969 Corvette Stingray Coupe, black exterior/interior, 427 cubic engine V8, 82,000 miles. Hot looking and definitely spirited. Contact owner."
Jim finally sold the car to a nice retired heterosexual couple from Connecticut. They really loved the car.

White Wash by Andrew V. Zourides

It was a quiet and still Friday afternoon in September 1958 in Sommerville, and Kurt lit up another cigarette. He looked at the car showroom's windows across the street and he knew that tomorrow they would be cleaned and the new 1959 cars would gleam in the sunlight much like the chromed trophies neatly shelved in his room. Not so prominently displayed, but hidden behind a chest, were his *other* objects of desire: scantily clad pictures of men. Pictures that were taken from muscle magazines and an occasional National Geographic.

He was seventeen, athletic, but not a "team" player and tended to be distant, a loner, and had a brooding disposition towards others. He inherited the best of features from his mother, that being his almond shaped bedroom eyes and flashing smile and his father's aquiline nose, strong chiseled chin and body. He was decidedly ethnic and unconventional for a small town population.

The fair was in town and he really wanted to go, but not alone as he had done before, but with a friend he had fantasized about…his friend Mike. Kurt thought of that last summer they drove to the lake in Mike's 1953 Mercury. After a swim, Mike snuck up from behind Kurt in the water, and in a quick instant put his powerful arms around him in a bear hug and lifted him out of the water, finally wrestling him onto the grassy embankment. That night, they had talked about what plans they had for the summer, baseball, and of course cars that they dreamed of having but as yet could never afford. This summer would be different. Kurt now had a plan, and decided he would take Mike to the fair, have some beers, and then drive to the lake, late that night. Maybe something, anything, would happen this time.

" I think you missed a spot, there near the back fender." Mike said teasingly. "You know you're going to wear off the paint if you polish it anymore."

Kurt smiled and with both hands held the towel taught and snapped it on Mike's ass.

"If you were a good friend, you'd help me with it next time. You borrowed it enough times you know."

Mike leaned against Kurt's car in the garage, a '55 Chevy Bel Air, and stretched putting his hands behind his head and showing off those powerful arms against the stark white tee. Coupled with the worn jeans and thick black belt, Kurt glanced nervously away. Mike noticing this, held Kurt's glance and took his fingers and slowly ran them along the sleek chromed edge of the car as if caressing it.

"You want to go to the fair tonight? It would be a lot of fun, don't you think?"

"I'm game. I'll sneak some beers from my Dad's shed. He won't miss them. He's half crocked anyway most of the time. I'll pick you up at seven. O.K.?"

Kurt wrapped the beers carefully in a towel and placed them in the trunk of the car that night and left as he had planned.

They had a great time at the fair hitting targets that tested their strength and skills and going on fast rides. Kurt imagined Mike looking at him sexually whenever his back was towards him and brushed accidently him any chance he could. He sat in the car while Mike relieved himself of all those beers, behind some bushes. He gazed hypnotically at the garish circle of lights from the carousel as they went around and around. He felt frustrated and sad about his feelings for Mike and the charade he was going through. He quickly turned on the radio and "Last Kiss" was playing about the fatal car wreck between two lovers.

"O.K. I'm done. Let's go to the lake and cool off." Mike said with new enthusiasm as he arched his legs and zipped up his jeans.

The lake was just a fifteen minute drive and Kurt was anxious under the haze of beers he just consumed. The lake was still and deserted as they slipped off their clothing and glided into the dark water.

"You left the headlights on in the car, dumb ass. I'll go back and turn them off. Stay here."

With that, Mike turned for the embankment and made for the car. Naked and wet, his body glistened from the headlights and he shivered from the sudden chill. Leaning into the car, he reached for the headlight switch and spread his white ass cheeks against the darkness.

Kurt had followed and found himself behind Mike and when Mike turned, he was literally face to face with him.

"I really needed a cigarette, Mike. They're in the glove compartment. Let me get them."

This time Kurt placed his hand on Mike's shoulder and balance his body while he strained to reach the glove compartment. He then felt Mike's warm tongue, licking along the back of his spine while his hand slowly stroked his right thigh. They both dropped to he ground and Kurt found his head propped against the front white wall tire as Mike laid his body firmly against him. Kurt grabbed the edges of the tire as they made love. The scent of sweat and rubber mixed with that of beer and cigarettes. His neck hurt from the hubcap's edge, but the taste and pleasure from Mike's lips made it all the more bearable.

The silence came back on the lake, and Kurt knew that nothing would be the same between Mike and him ever again. His mind wandered back again to the image of the carousel, the music and the bright lights. He wished he was a child, again carefree, grabbing tightly on the reigns of the horses, slipping slowly to its side.

Saturday came and they removed the white wash from the showroom windows. Mike lit his cigarette, put it to his lips, drew on it, and then offered it to Kurt, and smiled.

Photography by Andrew V. Zourides

Harder They Fall

The wind blew cool and heavy with moisture that late August night in Provincetown. Jason's 1971 Buick Riviera was parked far in the east end and suspended droplets had formed completely enveloping the copper toned vehicle. Perspiration dripped from Jason's forehead and clung to his damp tee shirt as he quickly wiped down the front and rear windshields. He was late again. The dinner party for ten guests was set for 8 o'clock and it was now half past. He had heard that Jacques was to be presently invited. Jacques was a 23 year old from Vermont and belonged to a gay wrestling team and was comfortable with his masculinity as he was unpretentious. That could hardly be the case for most present at the dinner party that evening. He had been waiting tables at two local restaurants all that summer and Jason had made it a point to eat at both of them. He had also gained six pounds. A man in his mid forties, he still wore it well on his six foot athletic frame. He still bore a small scar on his forehead from a nearly fatal car accident. The Buick Riviera was a well deserved gift to himself for five years of sobriety.
"I am really sorry that I am late, Ted. I hope you started without me."

"Actually, everyone is still on their cocktails. Not to worry, Ted, *and* Jacques has been asking about you. Are you alright? You look a bit piqued."

Jason was still tense and dehydrated from the anxiety he placed on himself from the late arrival.

"Just a cranberry drink with a twist of lemon will do just fine, Ted. Thanks."

Jacques was cornered near the fireplace by an interested suitor, but glanced over to Jason, winked and smiled.

Jason gratefully found himself seated besides Jacques at the dinner placing.

"This is great! We *finally* get to sit with each other instead of me standing, telling you the specials." Jacques said, holding Jason's gaze with a warm, inviting smile. Jason's face lit up from the undivided attention.

"I've enjoyed every special you suggested. Jason paused then said: "Well, you have a convincing smile… What are your plans?" Are you going back to Vermont after the season?"

"Not for awhile. I've got a shot at starting a landscaping business in Vermont with a friend. We should start in October and go full swing by spring."

"Good plan. But I will have to say I will miss you here in the summers."

Jacques, not taking his eyes from the plate, responded:

"You needn't be I will always make time to come to P-town. It's a very special place to me. My family used to drive down their old Buick when I was a child. By the way, where is that huge car of yours? Parking is impossible here especially in the west end."

"She's parked up on the hill by the dunes. I got here kind of late."

You know I'd love to go for a ride...*maybe* we could go dancing and work off dinner at the A-House later tonight?" Jacques had a playful and devilish way of convincing anyone. Jason gladly agreed with visions of a hot and sweaty encounter on the dance floor of the A-House. His heart sank at the thought of being immersed in a totally alcoholic environment. He had not been in a bar for just that reason for nearly a year now. He remembered the sense of thoughtless abandonment he felt when he drank and the sting of regret afterwards.

The pulsating beat quickened and the mirrored ball spun as it had for him some twenty years before. He was Jacques age then, and the strobe lit scene had become all too familiar. Jacques removed his shirt with a confident ease, only to reveal a portion of his red wrestling uniform underneath. It was certainly a welcome surprise to Jason, who would have gladly been pinned over and over again by such a beautiful man only to recite "I submit" as if it were a silent prayer.

Last call found them bathed in the harsh light of the overhead lamps revealing the night's revelers. The crowd was sweaty and stoned, some were exhausted while others were seeking a second high.

Let's get out of here <u>now</u>. Jacques tugged firmly at Jason's arm inexorably pulling him towards the exit, passing the tightly packed and smoky crowd.

The Buick Riviera vied for attention in the parking lot under the guise of the looming granite Pilgrim's Monument.

"That is definitely a cool looking car. I love the rear look of that car. It looks like the rear of a '63 Sting Ray." His animated and heighted speech was slurred down by the doses of alcohol.

"And I love *your* rear, Jason softly growled. It looks like a 2001 Bubble Butt."

Jacques grinned and shrugged. As high as he was, he said nothing of the obvious cheesy remark.

They drove back to the quieter part of the west end of town where Jacques lived for the duration of the summer. Jason pulled up to the darkened house and parked. It was late and the only sound was that of the waves gently breaking on the moorings.

"Stay here in the car and I'll tell you when to come up…O.K.?"

Jason could here him stumble up the stairs and then there was silence.

Jason felt odd, but sat alone in the Buick for at least ten minutes and found himself nervously tapping on the vinyl clad steering wheel.

"What the hell is he doing in there?" He said under his breath.

He shifted out of the car and onto the darkened deck of the house. The door was ajar and he could faintly make out the flickering candles in the hallway.

"Jacques? Are you there? Jacques?"

The staircase was steep, as many were in the older homes of Provincetown. It grew darker the further he ascended and he was startled by the quick movement of cats crossing his path, purring and beckoning him upwards.

The landing appeared from the darkness as did a figure leaning against an arched doorway. The peculiar smell of sweet incense filled the air of the landing.

"Jacques, is that you?" Jason now pronounced in a louder, but anxious tone.

Jason was apprehensive and felt something was wrong with the whole scene. Suddenly the figure lunged at him, wrestling him to the floor. Jason could see that it was Jacques, all over him, tearing at his clothes while grinding Jason's crotch with his own. He could feel his hard, worked body under the wrestling suit as Jacques wrapped his muscled legs around his thighs.

"Got you where I want you, big guy…bet you didn't expect *this* from a little guy like me, huh?"

The groping and wrestling moved onto hotter love making in the adjacent room where Jacques had placed softly lit candles. Stark contrast to the aggressive move set some ten minutes before.

At a cool 46, Jason knew and had perfected some of his own lovemaking moves that left the cocky youngster pleasantly surprised.

That morning, Jason reluctantly departed, exchanging the obligatory phone numbers and emails between them. They promised to keep in touch, though soon, they would be many miles apart.

As Jason parked the Riviera at his home outside Boston, he only then realized how sore his body was from the erotic workout. Opening the glove compartment, he found a crumpled beige plastic bag. In it, to his amazement, was the red wrestling suit with a little note attached to the crotch. It read:

"Two out of three falls? Winner takes all."
Jason held the uniform to his face, smiled and turned off the ignition.

Andrew with Santa 1956
Vintage Photograph from personal collection

Snapshot

"Where would you like me to hang the balls, honey?"

Hector asked in a low sexy voice, as he was perched high on top of a ladder.

"Anywhere, as long as they are above my head, hang low and they are where I can grab them."

Chris answered, trying to contain his laughter.

This was now going to be the fourth Christmas they will have spent together in Brooklyn since they met in 1972. Hector loved the holidays and always decorated the apartment as if he were decorating the windows at Bloomingdales. Chris didn't interfere much and besides, he wasn't very good at decorating as he was at fixing cars. His car, a 1960 Chevy Impala with gull wing fins, sat quietly in a rented garage down the block.

Hector was of Cuban descent and had strikingly fine features. Green grey eyes and thick, jet black hair with a disarming smile to boot. He possessed a smooth cool sensuality bred from constant workouts and meticulous grooming. Chris, on the other hand, was to validate the notion and cliché, which opposites, do attract. He had always the look of afternoon sleep in his eyes, unruly brown, curly hair that framed his rugged features and he wore a more casual appearance overall. He was very handsome and totally unaware of his beauty. Hector <u>loved</u> that quality and Hector, in return, truly loved him.

Donna Summer continued to wail from the radio that day, as the Christmas decorations filled the living room of the Brooklyn brownstone. It was exactly a week before Christmas.

"I can't believe how quickly the day went doing all these decorations. I really can't." Hector sighed in disbelief. "We better get our asses in high gear so we can make the party by eight. Hector scanned the room.

"Where *is* your Santa outfit?"

"Where ever you put it last, Hector. But I did find the hat, though."

There Chris stood, in the arched doorway. He was naked except for a pair of white socks and the red Santa hat, and wearing a wide, devilish grin.

"God, why didn't Santa look like you when I was a kid? I would have NEVER left his lap!"

43

Hector, tightly clad in polyester black, began to slowly kiss Chris' face, neck and his shoulders, excited by his coarse hairs on his chest and late afternoon beard. If they made love now, he thought, a quick one would be such a tease and a long hot passionate one would mean ultimately, a very late entrance. So, what the hell...Why not be fashionably late? To that they quickly undressed and dropped to the floor forming a tangled pile of red and white cotton and black polyester clothing beside them. Afterwards, they just lay side by side, exhausted, sprawled out on the living room rug.

"Here are the keys to the car. You just start it up while I look for the Santa suit. Knowing *you*, it has to be hanging neatly in one of the closets."

Hector grabbed his coat and keys and flew out the door. Chris was to find the Santa outfit, as expected, neatly pressed but hanging behind the bedroom door. Quickly he dressed, threw the gifts in a shopping bag, and slammed the door shut behind him.

Hector sat there in the darkened garage, turning the ignition key to the Impala, over and over again. The Impala shook and groaned, and then went dead.

"Why don't we get a Pacer, like Doug and Ted have, and get rid of this museum heap? Who has an AM radio anymore anyway? You know I like to listen to Donna Summer and disco on the radio and all I can get is that damn Do-Wop!"

Hector's face was clearly agitated as he looked straight ahead and not at Chris.

"The Impala is already considered a classic car and the crappy Pacer is not, and never will be! It is as simple as that!"

"All I know that we are late for the party and your car won't start! Here are the keys and *you* give it a try, moron!"

Visibly perturbed Chris got out of the car and into the driver's seat. He removed the Santa hat, and then slowly turned the ignition key. The Impala was *his* baby, and he knew to put a gentle, but steady pressure on the gas pedal and coax her into starting. The Impala gave a deep growl at first, then lowered to a soft purr and coasted along. The grand machine seemed so out of place all dressed up in turquoise and chrome in a dark, drafty garage in Brooklyn and in the dead of winter.

Hector looked at Chris as the anger left his face and he became collectively calmer. In complete silence they drove onto the icy streets towards the Brooklyn Queens Expressway and Long Island. Hector placed his hand on Chris' right leg and gently squeezed it in an effort to say he was sorry. He knew how much he loved the Impala and besides, Donna summer sounded just great on vinyl, but didn't look as hot in a Santa suit.

The Christmas party on Long Island, that year in 1976, was a big success and Chris' Santa outfit was a definite hit. The suit eventually came off after a few too many drinks, as Santa did a slow, raunchy strip tease to Jingle Bell Rock.

The years had passed and Chris was now gone, a sad casualty of the early 1980's. His suit still hangs in Hector's closet, neatly pressed, with a Polaroid of the Impala pinned to the fur trimmed hat.

Photography by Andrew V. Zourides

Stranded

It was a hot and overcast late afternoon, a week after Labor Day. Brad had found himself stranded at the far end of the beach, without a ride and few prospects. His friend was no where to be found except for the damp and twisted orange towel now half buried in the sand. He headed for the parking lot, about a mile up the beach, and hopefully he could hook up with a ride somehow.

He had a lean handsome face that was made more apparent from the recently cropped haircut he had. Fair in complexion, he was now sunburned on his face and neck making his eyes painfully blue. His cutoff jeans were caked in sand, as well as his thick legs and calves from his love of biking. His 19th birthday went unnoticed and he had hoped that he had saved enough money to put a down payment on the plum Crazy Dodge Charger he loved. It would be his gift to himself.

"Hey man, you look like you're in a daze." Brad looked up and perched between two sand dunes was a dark haired guy that seemed vaguely familiar to him. He slid down the dune confidently towards him, keeping his balance as the sands shifted beneath him.

"Hi, I met you before. You're Rick's friend aren't you?"

Brad then remembered meeting him briefly at the pool party earlier that summer and had found him interesting to talk to. Besides, he had long thick black hair and a beard. Brad had a thing for dark men with beards.

"Yeah, I am, and my so called *friend* has also left me here with no way back with out a car. We must have gotten our wires crossed as to who I was leaving with, I guess."

"I was getting ready to leave soon also. I'll drive you. I pass Hillside on the way. I remember you were telling me at the party that you lived there. By the way, my name is Zach."

Brad still had the look of surprise that he had remembered where he lived. He was glad that he must have made an impression to Zach.

"Mine's Brad, and I do remember you from the party."

With that, Brad shook hands while Zach put the other hand on Brad's shoulder, and squeezed it. He had such intense eyes, that for one embarrassing moment, Brad just stood there motionless.

It had gotten late and there, at the far corner of the now empty parking lot, was Zach's red 1964 Plymouth Barracuda. Brad had always liked the car, and his older cousin had owned one. A bearded cousin, no less, and that he had always fantasized about.

"Nice car. I always like that large rear window. The seats fold down, don't they?"

Brad had a sly grin when he said it, which intentionally gave away his double meaning.

"Yeah, I guess it can hold two people, but it can get really hot in there."

Another innuendo and this time Zach was the one flashing the smile.

Brad noticed the odd hood ornament and commented that it was really cool. It was a chromed devil, thumbing the world with his hand to his nose.

"I thought it was cool looking and I picked it up at a flea market."

At that moment, the skies opened up in a torrential downpour. They quickly went into the car and sat silent. The dash and interior were glossy red and matte silver, and as Brad looked at Zach's profile against it, he thought of the devil hood ornament thumbing his hand at the world. Zach seemed like he would do just that. His hair was dark and thick and fell in locks on the nape of his neck. Shirtless, Brad had noticed his smooth broad shoulders as he hunched over the wheel. He reached over and brushed a small patch of sand that clung to the center of Zach's shoulder blades. The particles of sand fell and drifted as from an hourglass, down the crack of his ass, which was exposed from his loose jeans.

The rain pelted the glass and now was coming down in sheets. Zach leaned over and placed his hand behind Brad's neck, pulling him forward and then softly kissed him, gently biting his lower lip. They both turned simultaneously and looked over their shoulders and smiled knowing that they were sharing the same thought. Zach reached back, the back seats flung forward, the bodies lunged, and droplets soon formed on the inside of the expansive rear window of that red Barracuda.

They saw each other for awhile after, and slowly, the intensity of the relationship on Zach's behalf, slacked off. They lost touch eventually and Brad had heard that Zach had moved to the West coast to some small town near San Francisco. Brad had always remembered his smile, his dark beard, and how his smooth skin felt like silk wrapped around steel.

48

Years had passed, ten to be exact. Brad had always loved to go to flea markets and would take pictures of objects he found of interest. It could also be an opportunity to meet a guy who was browsing, and what was wrong with that?

He came upon one vendor, a woman with a large brimmed hat, selling a table filled with Victorian glass. There parked behind her table, his eyes fixed upon a chromed devil hood ornament poised on the hood of a 1964 Plymouth Barracuda. The red paint had faded but the devil still glittered in the strong sunlight. He asked where she had gotten the car and she replied that she bought it years ago, from a young man who was moving to California.

Brad stepped back, took his camera in hand, and snapped the picture.